AF605701

Migration to Australia

Refugees

William Day

First published 2017 by
Redback Publishing
PO Box 357 Frenchs Forest NSW 2086
Australia

978-1-925630-11-4

Author: William Day
Editor: Margie Tubbs
Designer: Redback Publishing

Original illustrations © Redback Publishing 2017
Originated by Redback Publishing

Printed and bound in China by Leo Paper

Acknowledgements
Abbreviations: l—left, r—right, b—bottom, t—top, c—centre, m—middle
We would like to thank the following for permission to reproduce photographs: (Images © shutterstock) front cover Sadik Gulec, p2 Sadik Gulec, p4 Janossy Gergely, p8 BalkansCat, p9 Zeljko Sinobad, p10 Anjo Kan, p12 Melih Cevdet Teksen, p13 TK Kurikawa, p15 OPIS Zagreb, p19t reinaimaging, p19b Nils Versemann, p25 Northfoto, p27 Sadik Gulec, p29 Orlok, p30 Bill Ragan,

Every effort has been made to contact copyright holders of any material reproduced in this book. Any omissions will be rectified in subsequent printings if notice is given to the publisher.

National Library of Australia Cataloguing-in-Publication entry

Creator: Day, William, author.
Title: Refugees / William Day.
ISBN: 9781925630114 (hardback)
Series: Migration to Australia.
Target Audience: For Primary school age.
Subjects: Refugees--Australia--History.
Refugees--Australia--Juvenile literature.

Contents

Refugees and Australia

Australia has been accepting refugees as settlers from colonial times up until the present. In the 1800s, each colonial government decided which refugees it would take and what degree of assistance it would provide for them.

As Australia confirmed its place in world affairs after World War II, it accepted thousands of displaced people.

After the creation of the United Nations and the UNHCR, refugee movements around the world, including to Australia, have been organised by individual member nations in consultation with the United Nations and its regulations.

Recent conflict in the Middle East has resulted in the largest movement of asylum seekers and displaced people since the end of World War II in 1945.

How You Can Help

The Australian Government recommends that Australians who want to help new arrivals should think about joining one of the volunteer organisations that work with refugees.

1951 Refugee Convention

Australia is one of the nations that have agreed to the standards laid down in the United Nations 1951 Refugee Convention. This agreement provides rules for the way in which refugees should be treated. It also defines exactly what the term 'refugee' means:

> *'A refugee is a person who is outside their own country and fears persecution based on their race, religion, nationality, social group or politics if they return.'*

Australia and the other countries that have agreed to the 1951 Refugee Convention are obliged to abide by its rules regarding people who are found to be genuine refugees. A refugee must not be returned to a country where their life or freedom will be threatened.

Other rights which the 1951 Refugee Convention states should be granted to a person, as long as they remain a refugee:

- The right to work
- The right to have housing, education and welfare
- The right to freedom of religion
- The right to freedom of movement
- Access to the courts and legal system
- The right to have an identity and travel document

The 1967 Protocol

The1967 Protocol is an amendment to the 1951 Refugee Convention. It allows the UNHCR to assist refugees beyond the countries of Europe. Australia has agreed to uphold the1967 Protocol.

Frequently Asked Questions

What is an asylum seeker?

Asylum seekers are people whose claims for refugee status have not yet been checked for their veracity and whose character and health checks have not been completed. The UNHCR rules offer approved refugees many protections and benefits that are not available to asylum seekers.

What is a displaced person?

A person who is still in their own country but who has had to leave their home in search of safety.

Is a migrant a refugee?

Migrants are not refugees, as they can choose to leave their country and continue to have the protection of their own government when they do so.

How long does a person remain a refugee?

For as long as the conditions in their own country remain dangerous for them, or until they are allowed to stay permanently in their host country.

Who does not qualify as a refugee?

War criminals or other people guilty of serious crimes.

What are the responsibilities of a refugee?

To abide by the law of their host country, and respect measures taken for public order.

Who decides if a person is a refugee?

A host country in consultation with the UNHCR.

How many refugees are there around the world?

1951 - 1.5 million
1980 - 8 million
2007 - 11 million
2008 - 15 million
2015 - 21 million

Australian Human Rights Commission Report (2013)

'Australia has resettled around 800,000 refugees since World War II, building one of the world's most successful multicultural societies. Today, Australia continues to have a generous resettlement program and, along with the United States and Canada, has ranked consistently among the world's top three resettlement countries.'

Top three nations accepting refugees for resettlement in 2011:

- USA - 51,500
- Canada - 12,900
- Australia - 9,200

Australia's Humanitarian Program

Australia's Humanitarian Program assists people still in areas of conflict and those who are in refugee camps outside their own countries. This aid includes providing food, shelter, water, education, health care and sewerage. In 2011, the largest proportion of humanitarian aid was given to assist Syrians still in Syria. The next highest amount of aid was given to help Syrian refugees who were living in Lebanon and Jordan.

Australia also offers a fixed number of humanitarian places each year for people who will be resettled in Australia. Before being granted a visa, refugees undergo health, character and security checks. These visas will not be granted to people who attempt to travel to Australia by boat without being approved beforehand.

People accepted as humanitarian settlers are granted permanent resident status, with all the rights and responsibilities of any other permanent resident who was not a refugee.

United Nations High Commission on Refugees (UNHCR)

Australia works with the UNHCR to determine which refugees are the most vulnerable and in greatest need of resettlement.

The UNHCR was established in 1950 to deal with the millions of refugees in Europe who had been forced to leave their homes during World War II. Since then, the UNHCR has assisted 50 million refugees around the world. It has over 10,000 staff members who work in 128 countries. The UNHCR receives its funding mostly from governments around the world.

In 2015, the UNHCR estimated there were 65 million people around the world who were forced to leave their homes due to war or persecution and became either refugees or displaced persons in their own countries.

Australian Aid

Australian aid overseas is delivered through a variety of organisations:

- The United Nations
- Humanitarian organisations such as the Red Cross
- Non-Government Organisations (NGOs)

Critical Needs of Refugees and Displaced Persons

The UNHCR identifies the following critical needs of refugees and displaced persons:

- Child protection
- Education
- Health
- Water and sanitation
- Determining a person's refugee status
- Having no country or state to protect them

Australian Civilian Corps (ACC)

The ACC was formed in 2011. Its purpose is to improve the Australian government's assistance to countries suffering disasters and conflict. A group of civilian specialists is always on standby, ready to be sent to places where their expertise can assist people in distress.

Boat People

The term 'boat people' was first used in the 1970s to refer to South Vietnamese refugees who fled when North Vietnamese forces took control of South Vietnam. People who did not support the new government in Vietnam feared reprisals and boarded small boats trying to reach places where they would be safe. About 2,000 Vietnamese boat people journeyed to Australia seeking asylum.

From 1999 onwards, people from Middle Eastern countries became the new boat people. Their boat trips to Australia have usually been organised by people smugglers. Thousands of boat people from Vietnam and the Middle East drowned when their small, unseaworthy boats sank.

The Australian government no longer allows boat people who arrive illegally to obtain a visa to stay in Australia.

People Smugglers

People smugglers are criminals who organise the boats and crew seeking to bring asylum seekers and illegal arrivals to Australia. The smugglers charge their passengers very large amounts of money. In Australia, people smuggling is a crime punishable with imprisonment.

Operation Sovereign Borders (OSB)

OSB is a military operation which aims to stop maritime people smuggling and to secure Australia's borders.

Detention Centres

It is mandatory under the Migration Act for every non-citizen who is in Australia without a valid visa to be detained. People placed in detention centres include asylum seekers, illegal arrivals and anyone whose visa has expired or been cancelled.

Nauru and Manus Island (Papua New Guinea)

Australia has agreements with the governments of these islands to house asylum seekers who have tried to reach Australia by boat and who do not have a valid visa.

Tampa Incident

In 2001, a Norwegian ship, the Tampa, rescued 433 boat people from their sinking vessel. The Tampa was not allowed to unload its passengers, who were eventually taken into detention on the island of Nauru.

Christmas Island

Christmas Island is an Australian Territory in the Indian Ocean to the northwest of the Australian mainland. It was the destination for many boat people. A large detention centre was built there.

Refugees after World War II

After World War II ended in 1945, Australia welcomed thousands of European refugees and displaced people. Between 1947 and 1954, 170,000 people left camps in Europe to settle in Australia.

Australia had a number of reasons for encouraging these post-war settlers:

- Australia had a small population at the time and the new arrivals eased labour shortages.
- Western governments feared the growth of communism in the Soviet Union and China. The new migrants were mostly anti-communist in their views and were therefore welcome in the community.
- The threat of invasion by Japan during World War II led the government to pay attention to the need to increase the population to make Australia more secure.

Migrant Hostels

Before the 1970s, refugees and new migrants were initially housed in migrant hostels. The largest were at Bonegilla in Victoria and Bathurst in New South Wales. The Villawood Migrant Hostel in Sydney was the first accommodation offered to many of the Vietnamese refugees in the 1970s.

Where Did They Come From?

Afghanistan

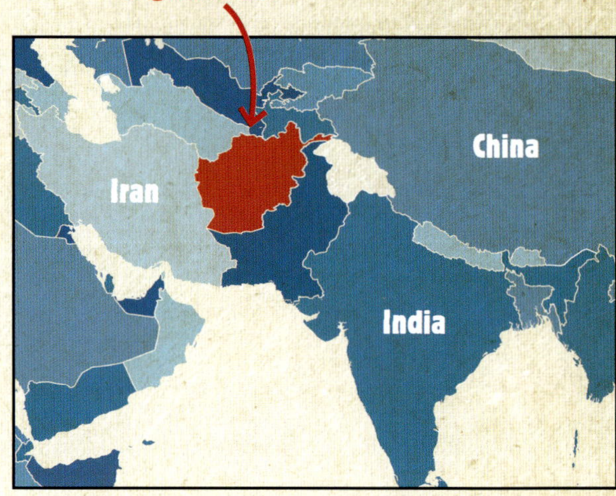

Where is Afghanistan?

Afghanistan is in the Middle East.

When did Afghan asylum seekers arrive in Australia?

- After 1979

Why were they seeking asylum?

In 1979, the Soviet Union invaded Afghanistan and stayed for ten years. When the Soviet Union withdrew its army, the Taliban seized the capital, Kabul, imposing a strict rule on the population. The civil war in Afghanistan has resulted in many Afghan people fleeing their country. A recent severe drought has made the living conditions there even worse. The Australian government advises against any travel to Afghanistan, stressing the dangerous situation that exists there.

Chile

Where is Chile?

Chile is in South America.

When did Chilean asylum seekers arrive in Australia?

- After 1973

Why were they seeking asylum?

Civil unrest occurred in Chile in 1973, when the government was overthrown in a military coup. Australia accepted a group of Chilean political refugees at this time.

China

Where is China?
China is in East Asia.

When did Chinese asylum seekers arrive in Australia?

- During World War II
- After 1949
- 1989

Why were they seeking asylum?
During World War II, Japan invaded China and occupied the coastal cities. Chinese people who were visiting Australia at the time, or who were sailors on merchant ships, could not go home and became refugees.

Although Australia had a White Australia Policy at the time, restricting the arrival of people based on their race, the government allowed these Chinese refugees to stay in Australia temporarily. After the war ended in 1945, most of the Chinese refugees had to return to China. A few were allowed to stay in Australia, where they started families and ran successful businesses.

When the People's Republic of China was declared in 1949, Chinese people who had not supported the communist movement feared for their safety. Some of them sought asylum in Australia.

In 1989, the Chinese government used tanks and soldiers to stop a large protest held in Tiananmen Square in Beijing. As a result of this action, Australia received thousands of requests for asylum from Chinese students who were studying in Australia.

inatown, Melbourne

Cyprus

Where is Cyprus?
Cyprus is an island in the Mediterranean Sea.

When did Cypriot asylum seekers arrive in Australia?

- After 1974

Why were they seeking asylum?
In 1974, Turkey occupied northern Cyprus. Greek Cypriots living in the north were expelled and became homeless. Many sought safety in other countries, including Australia.

Czechoslovakia

Where is Czechoslovakia?
Czechoslovakia was the name of a country in central Europe. In 1993, the country split into the Czech Republic and the Slovak Republic.

When did Czechoslovakian asylum seekers arrive in Australia?

- After World War II
- From 1968

Why were they seeking asylum?
During World War II, Czechoslovakia was annexed by Germany. Many Czechoslovakian people sought refuge in other countries. After the war, Australia accepted thousands of Czechoslovakians as refugees.

In 1968, Czechoslovakia was invaded by the Soviet Union. Australia again accepted the displaced people as refugees, this time taking about 6,000 Czechoslovakians for resettlement.

East Timor

Where is East Timor?
East Timor is an island to the northwest of Australia.

When did East Timorese asylum seekers arrive in Australia?

- From 1975 onwards

Why were they seeking asylum?
Indonesia opposed East Timor's independence and invaded in 1975. A civil war began between people who opposed independence and those who supported it. 2,500 asylum seekers arrived in Darwin in 1975 from East Timor. Some of them were transferred to Portugal but the majority were sent to hostels in Sydney and Melbourne. East Timor became an independent nation in 2002.

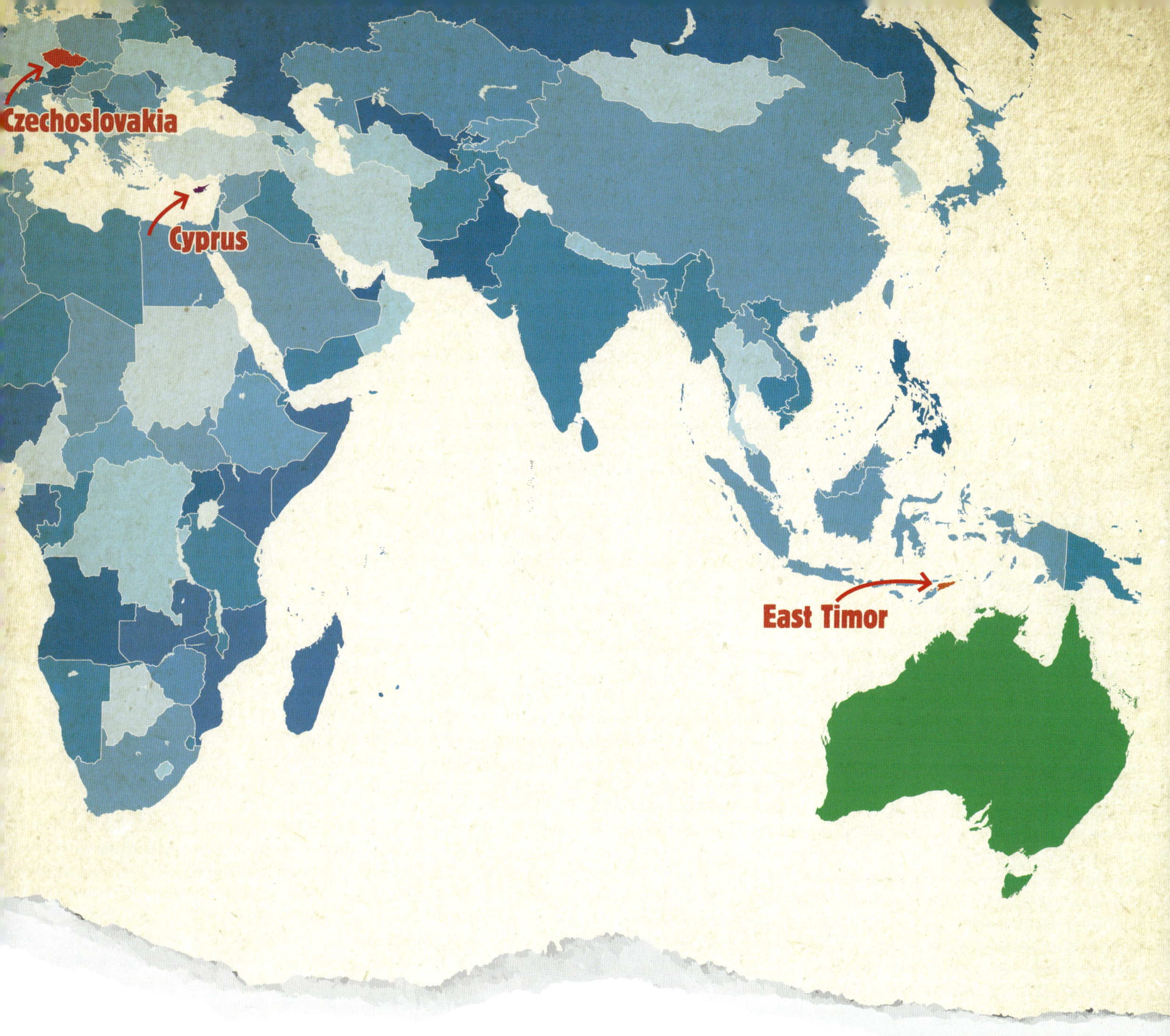

Colonial Government Response to Refugees

The colonial governments of Australia had no special refugee policies. They welcomed people from Europe to ease the labour shortages that were restricting economic development. The Commonwealth of Australia did not develop a formal refugee policy until the 1970s.

Germany

Where is Germany?
Germany is in central Europe.

When did German asylum seekers arrive in Australia?

- From the mid to late 1800s

Why were they seeking asylum?
There were two waves of German refugees who arrived in Australia in the colonial era. In the early 1800s, members of the Lutheran Church in Germany found it difficult to practise their religion freely. From the 1830s, many German Lutherans migrated to the Australian colonies where they could worship without restrictions.

The next wave of German refugees left their homeland from the 1850s onwards, due to growing political unrest and armed conflict. The German settlers mostly went to South Australia, where they developed the wine industry, built their Lutheran churches and left German place names as a reminder of their presence.

Hungary

Where is Hungary?
Hungary is in central Europe.

When did Hungarian asylum seekers arrive in Australia?

- After the late 1840s
- After World War I
- After World War II
- After the invasion of Hungary by the Soviets in 1956

Why were they seeking asylum?
Some Hungarian people left their country to find a better life after 1849 and after World War II

After World War II ended in 1945, Hungarians joined the millions of displaced European people seeking refuge in other countries, including Australia.

The Soviet Union moved into Hungary in 1956. Once again, some Hungarian people became refugees. This time they were assisted by the United Nations, which had set up refugee camps from which Australia accepted many Hungarian people.

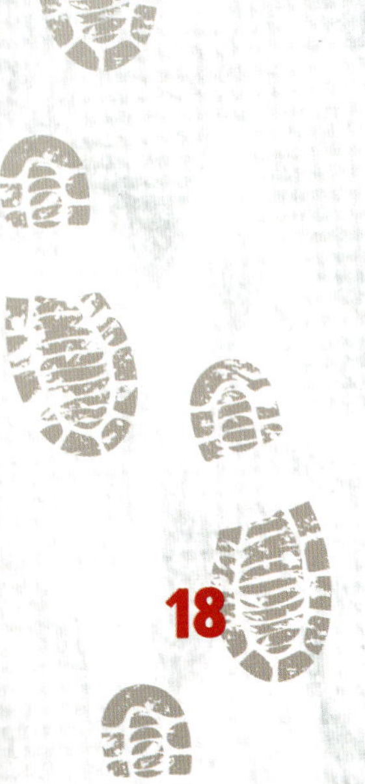

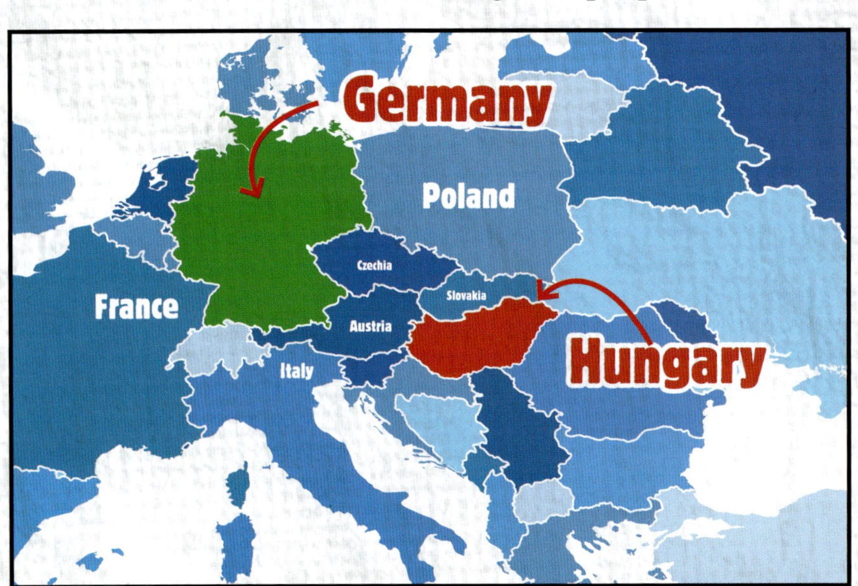

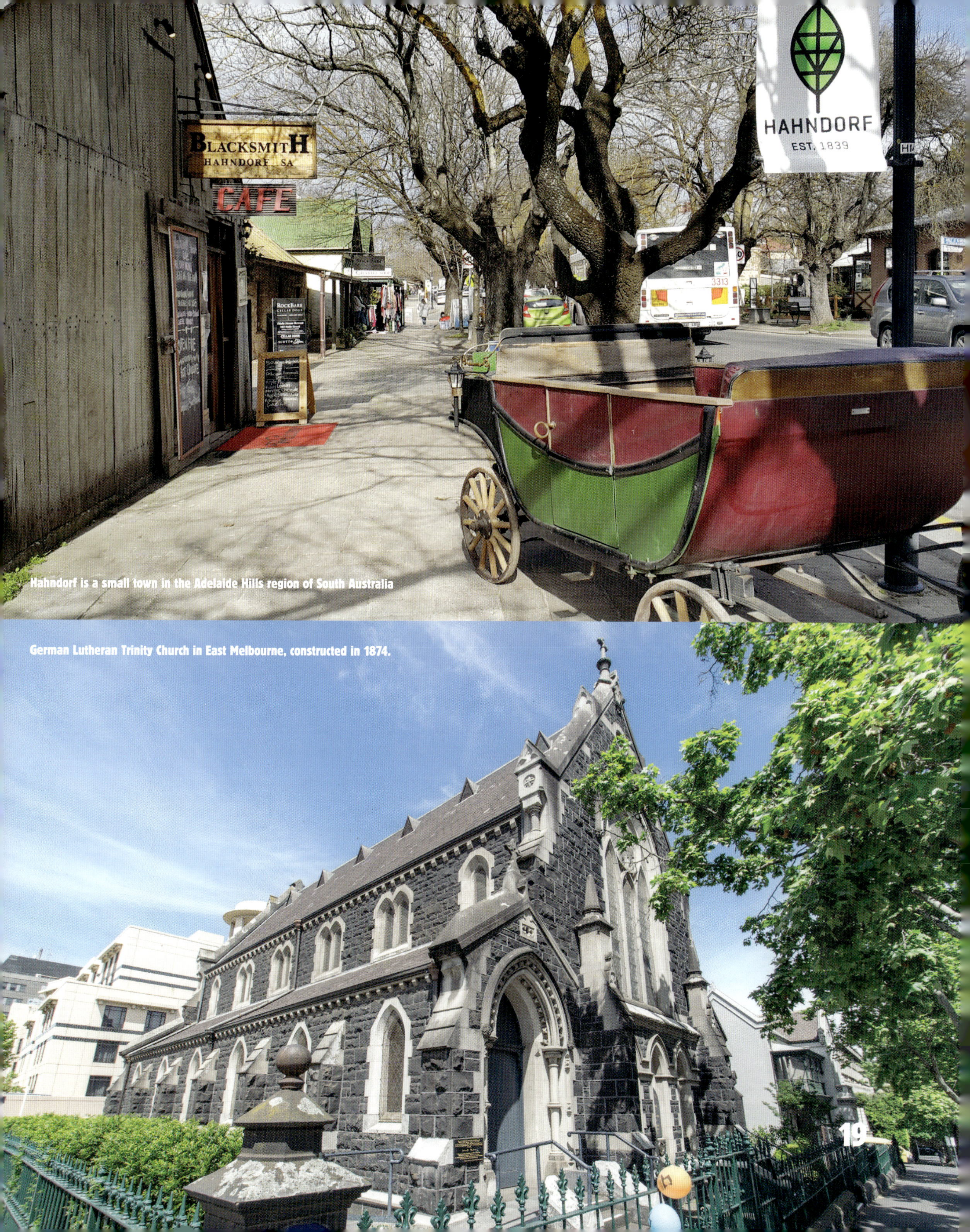

Hahndorf is a small town in the Adelaide Hills region of South Australia

German Lutheran Trinity Church in East Melbourne, constructed in 1874.

Iran

Where is Iran?
Iran is in the Middle East.

When did Iranian asylum seekers arrive in Australia?

- In the 1980s

Why were they seeking asylum?
In 1981, the Australian Government set up a Humanitarian Program to allow Iranian people of the Baha'i faith to settle in Australia. A new government had taken control of Iran in a revolution in 1979, and it did not permit people of the Baha'i faith to practise their religion freely.

Many more Iranian people sought to escape the strict religious government in Iran and the conflict during the war with Iraq in the 1980s.

Iraq

Where is Iraq?
Iraq is in the Middle East.

When did Iraqi asylum seekers arrive in Australia?

- From 1991

Why were they seeking asylum?
In 1991, the Gulf War resulted in thousands of Iraqi people being forced to leave their country and live in camps in neighbouring areas. Australia accepted a number of Iraqi refugees as part of its Humanitarian Program.

Italian immigrants

Italy

Where is Italy?

Italy is in southern Europe.

When did Italian asylum seekers arrive in Australia?

- In 1881
- After 1945

Why were they seeking asylum?

In 1880, a group of Italians were persuaded to pay the Marquis de Rays large amounts of money to settle in an idyllic township in Papua New Guinea. The scheme was a scam and there was no township. When Sir Henry Parkes heard about it in Australia, he sent a ship to collect the Italians and bring them to New South Wales. They arrived in 1881 and eventually formed a settlement called New Italy in northern New South Wales.

After the end of World War II in 1945, Italians were among the European refugees and displaced persons who travelled to Australia.

Jewish Refugees

When did Jewish asylum seekers arrive in Australia?

- Early1900s
- From the 1930s
- After World War II

Why were they seeking asylum?

Jewish people have sought asylum in Australia after fleeing religious persecution and displacement from their homes.

In the early 1900s, Jewish people were persecuted in Imperial Russia. Some left to find asylum in countries that would allow them to practise their religion with freedom.

From the 1930s, Adolf Hitler and the Nazi Party of Germany persecuted Jewish people, resulting in mass genocide. As Germany invaded or annexed more countries, their Jewish populations found that they were no longer safe. Some Jewish people managed to escape and travel to Australia.

Kosovo

Where is Kosovo?
Kosovo is in Eastern Europe.

When did Kosovan asylum seekers arrive in Australia?

- In 1999

Why were they seeking asylum?
Kosovo was involved in a war to gain independence from Serbia. Many people had to flee from their homes to escape the fighting. When the war ended, the United Nations administered Kosovo until a government could be formed.

In 1999, Australia accepted 4,000 temporary refugees from Kosovo and they were granted a three-month visa. They travelled by plane and were housed initially in disused army barracks in Tasmania. Most returned home when the war was over, helped by a resettlement allowance.

Lebanon

Where is Lebanon?
Lebanon is in the Middle East.

When did Lebanese asylum seekers arrive in Australia?

- From 1976

Why were they seeking asylum?
In 1975, a civil war in Lebanon resulted in the death or displacement of thousands of people. Many sought refuge in Australia, some joining family members who were already residents.

Much of Kosovo was destroyed during fighting with Serb forces.

What Is a Visa?

An official authority to enter and stay in a country for a defined length of time.

Poland

Where is Poland?
Poland is in central Europe.

When did Polish asylum seekers arrive in Australia?

- After World War II
- In the 1980s

Why were they seeking asylum?
After the end of World War II, some displaced persons from Poland went to Australia. Among them were Polish soldiers who had fought alongside British troops.

In the 1980s, Polish people came to Australia escaping the political unrest in Poland resulting from the movement for a democratic government and freedom from the USSR.

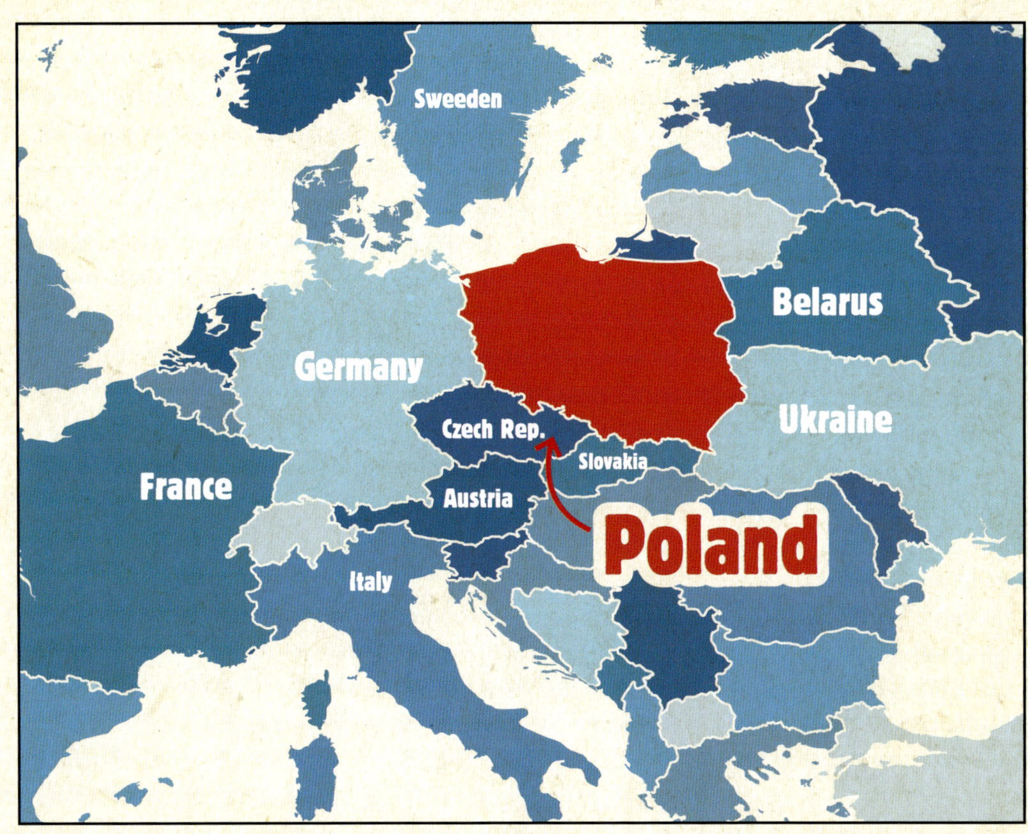

Somalia

Where is Somalia?
Somalia is in the Horn of Africa.

When did Somali asylum seekers arrive in Australia?

- From 1992

Why were they seeking asylum?
1n 1991, a civil war in Somalia resulted in the death or displacement of half the country's population. Many sought refuge in other countries. The largest number of Somali refugees to Australia settled in Victoria.

Sri Lanka

Where is Sri Lanka?
Formerly called Ceylon, Sri Lanka is an island to the south of India.

When did Sri Lankan asylum seekers arrive in Australia?

- From 1983

Why were they seeking asylum?
From 1983, ethnic conflict in Sri Lanka resulted in people seeking safety in other countries, including Australia.

Recent Asylum Seekers

Most of the people seeking asylum in Australia in 2012 came from Afghanistan, Sri Lanka, Iran, Pakistan and Iraq.

South Sudan and Sudan

Where is South Sudan?
South Sudan is in central Africa.

When did South Sudanese asylum seekers arrive in Australia?

- From 2001

Why were they seeking asylum?
Political disputes, civil war and drought have affected South Sudan for many years. The majority of South Sudanese refugees in Australia live in Victoria. They had fled to refugee camps in neighbouring countries, before being selected to settle in Australia.

Before 2011, South Sudan was a part of the country of Sudan. Separation in 2011 did not end the civil unrest, so asylum seekers from both countries left to wait in refugee camps for resettlement.

Syria

Where is Syria?
Syria is in the Middle East.

When did Syrian asylum seekers arrive in Australia?

- From 2011

Why were they seeking asylum?
In 2011, a civil war broke out in Syria. This war has resulted in the world's largest humanitarian crisis since World War II. Millions of Syrian people have been left homeless and many have sought safety in United Nations refugee camps in nearby countries. Some Syrians have tried to come to Australia by boat or have journeyed to countries in Western Europe, hoping they will be allowed to stay.

In 2015, the Australian Government increased the number of permanent visas it will offer to people fleeing as a result of the conflict in Syria and Iraq, and who are in camps in Turkey, Lebanon or Jordan.

Australia also provides assistance within Syria to help the people there. Funding to assist education aims to improve the future prospects of the Syrians, both in their own country and in other nearby places where they are living as refugees.

NSW Australian of the Year 2017

At the age of six, Deng Adut was forced to become a child soldier in Sudan. After escaping to a UN refugee camp in Kenya, he applied for a visa to enter Australia and arrived in 1998. Deng Adut studied for a law degree and now works for the welfare of the Sudanese community from his law practice in Western Sydney.

Vietnam

Where is Vietnam?
Vietnam is in Southeast Asia.

When did Vietnamese asylum seekers begin to arrive in Australia?

- In the late 1970s

Why were they seeking asylum?
The civil war in Vietnam was fought between people from the north and the south of the country. In 1975, communist North Vietnamese troops took the southern capital city, ending the war. People from the south feared persecution and death from the new regime, and they fled to other countries.

Vietnamese asylum seekers who arrived in Australia in the 1970s, after the end of the Vietnam War, were the first large-scale arrivals to come after the White Australia Policy ended. Some came as boat people, while others were selected from refugee camps in Southeast Asian countries.

Visit these websites to find out more about refugees:

www.humanrights.gov.au

www.unhcr.org

www.border.gov.au/Trav/Refu

Glossary

armed using weapons

civil war war in which people from the same country fight each other

communism political theory that involves people sharing wealth

genocide mass murder based on enthnicity

mandatory compulsory

maritime connected with the sea

merchant ships ships carrying goods for trade

military coup overthrow of a government by soldiers

to annex land to add a section of land to a nation

veracity truthfulness

Index